Vanished!

Tamim Ansary

Illustrations by Derrick Williams

1   2   3   4   5   6   7   8   9   10

ISBN 0-8250-4977-0

Copyright © 2004

Walch Publishing

P. O. Box 658 • Portland, Maine 04104-0658

walch.com

Printed in the United States of America

WALCH **PUBLISHING**

Vanished!

Table of Contents

Introduction

Every year, hundreds of people disappear. Some of them probably vanish on purpose. They get tired of their old lives. They want to start over. So they move to new cities. They change their names and their looks. They get new jobs. In this way, they become new people.

Others disappear because they are in trouble. They owe money or have powerful enemies. They need to hide. Some people disappear because their enemies catch up with them. They may be crime victims. Every big city police department has a "missing persons" section.

Some disappearances are too puzzling

even for the police. They may involve the disappearance of many people, not just one. Ships, planes, houses, and whole towns may disappear. Some of these disappearances are weird—even frightening.

The important thing is to get past the fear and look at the facts. A puzzling disappearance is like any other puzzle. When you fit the known facts together, you can often guess the unknown parts. Working out such puzzles is good practice. You can use the same skill to solve the puzzles in your own life. Instead of feeling helpless or confused by frightening events, you become an investigator. You may even make some of your problems . . . disappear.

In 1937, the Japanese invaded China. Six
months into the war, the big city of
Shanghai fell to them. Other nations spoke

out against the Japanese, but their words were useless. The Japanese pushed toward the heart of China. They began to march on Nanking, the capital. But the mighty Yangtze River stretched across their path. To reach Nanking, they would have to cross a narrow bridge. The Chinese commander, Colonel Li Fu Sien, decided to fight at that bridge. If he could stop the Japanese there, he just might save his country.

He had 3,000 men under his command. He made his soldiers dig a trench about a mile from the bridge. They set up their big guns in the trench. They lay down to wait. Around nightfall, the colonel took a last

look at his soldiers. They seemed ready for battle. The Japanese were sure to attack in the morning. The colonel went to his tent to get some sleep.

The next morning his aides woke him up. They were very nervous. Something strange was going on. They were trying to contact the 3,000 soldiers by radio and were getting no answer.

The colonel rode to the front line. To his great surprise, he found the trench empty. The big guns were there, but the men were gone.

They could not have run away. The river was at their backs. The only way across that

river was over the bridge. And on that bridge, there were sentries. None of them had seen or heard a thing. One or two soldiers might have slipped past them—but not 3,000.

Nor could the soldiers have run the other way. The Japanese army had them boxed in.  One or two Chinese soldiers could have slipped through the Japanese lines. But the whole army? Surely not!

Had the Japanese attacked during the night? Had they beaten

the Chinese soldiers and dragged them all away? That, too, seemed impossible. A battle is very noisy. Guns boom. People scream. Yet, the colonel and his aides had not heard any such sounds during the night. What, then, had happened to those 3,000 men? At the time, only two answers seemed possible. They must have gone over to the Japanese, or they must have quietly given up.

The colonel had no time to wonder about it. Suddenly, the Japanese were pouring over the hills. They crossed the river easily. They hit Nanking hard. Soon they ruled all of China. And soon after that, World War II broke out. Everyone forgot

about the mystery of the missing army.

After World War II, American officers looked through the Japanese army's records. It turned out the Japanese knew nothing about the missing men. They had been just as surprised as Colonel Sien to find them gone. To this day, no one knows what happened to all those men. They are simply listed as "missing in action."

This was not the first time a big group of soldiers had disappeared. An even more baffling case took place during World War I, at the Battle of Gallipoli. The Russians and the British were fighting the Turks in that battle. At one point, a regiment of

British soldiers was told to march over a certain hill. The Turks were waiting on the other side.

The British regiment was the First Norfolk. It numbered about 1,000 men. Hundreds of people watched them march up Hill 60. It was a clear summer afternoon. There was only one cloud in the sky. But that one cloud was resting on top of Hill 60. It looked as solid and heavy as a loaf of bread. The wind was shaking the leaves that day. But the cloud was not even stirring.

The first row of British soldiers moved

into the cloud. The second row marched in behind them. The third row marched in next. Row after row, the men kept marching into the cloud. No one came out the other side. When the cloud had taken in the last man, it drifted away. Below it, people saw an empty hill. The whole regiment had vanished like dry ice on a hot day.

People have come up with many ideas to explain these disappearances. Some say a spaceship took them all away. (But some people say this about every strange disappearance.) These people say the cloud had a spaceship inside it. Why would creatures from another planet steal 1,000 British soldiers? That's a good question.

Perhaps they were having a war of their own somewhere and needed some soldiers. Perhaps word had gotten around the universe: Earth has a lot of wars. Its soldiers must be tough.

Jerrold Potter had no reason to disappear. He was a happily married man with no enemies. He lived in the pleasant little town of Kankakee, Illinois, and made pretty good money. The townspeople liked him. He was not the type to go on any wild adventures.

Jerrold Potter belonged to the Lions Club, a men's club that does good deeds locally. In 1968, Jerrold and his wife, Carrie, decided to go to a Lions Club convention. It was being held in Dallas, Texas, that year. Potter and his wife planned the trip for months. It was *their* idea of a wild adventure.

On June 29, they boarded a DC-9 bound for Texas. The plane carried 22 passengers and two flight attendants.

Jerrold Potter

Somewhere over the Midwest, Mr. Potter went to the bathroom. His wife noticed him go, but she was sleepy and did not check the time. Other Lions from Kankakee were on the plane. They chatted with Mr. Potter as he made his way down the aisle. No one noticed him come back.

At one point, the plane hit a pocket of rough air. It dropped and then bounced back up. Such jolts are not unusual on long flights. But as time passed, Mrs. Potter began to worry about her husband. She thought he might have banged his head when the plane jolted. He might have knocked himself out. She called the flight attendant over and said, "Excuse me. My husband went to the bathroom quite a while ago. He's not back. Could you check on him, please?"

The flight attendant went to the back of the plane. She found both bathrooms empty. She searched for Mr. Potter and turned up no trace of him. She signaled the pilots that something was wrong. Copilot Roy Bacus ambled back. He heard the whole story. Then he searched the rear of the plane himself. He did spot something disturbing: The safety chain on the boarding gate was hanging loose.

In a modern jet, the doors cannot be opened when the plane is in the air. These

planes fly high up, where the air is thin. The doors are sealed. If they were to open, the air would rush out, sucking the people with it. But the DC-9 was a low-flying aircraft. It was not pressurized. The boarding gate could have been opened without making the plane crash.

Did Mr. Potter open the gate by accident? Did he mistake it for the bathroom door? Impossible. The gate was covered with huge red warning labels. Also, opening it was no simple matter. The long handle had to be turned completely around. Then two pins had to be removed. Then a safety chain had to be unhooked. Finally, the whole heavy door

had to be swung up on
hinges. On the
ground, the
two flight
attendants
working together
could not open it. A special crew was
assigned to the job. In the air, the gate
was even harder to open.

No, if Jerrold Potter opened that door,
he did it on purpose. And it's hard to
imagine how he could have gotten away
with it. The flight attendants were
constantly going to the rear of the plane
for supplies. Surely they would have
noticed a man struggling to open the

boarding gate.

But let's say Potter did open the gate. An even tougher question comes up. Why did he do it? He had no parachute. He must have known he would die if he left the plane in midair.

And yet, Jerrold Potter was gone. We know that much for sure, because the pilots landed as soon as they found out a passenger was missing. They landed at a small city in north Texas. Police and security experts rushed aboard. They searched every crack and crevice. Jerrold Potter was gone. His body was never found, either.

How can we explain this disappearance? Did someone forget to lock the boarding gate? Did it swing open just as Jerrold Potter was walking by? Or did someone leave the gate open on purpose? Perhaps there was a big plot to get rid of Potter. Did Potter have a secret life? Was he, perhaps, a spy?

There is another possibility. Maybe Potter wanted to disappear. Maybe he changed into a disguise in the bathroom. It could have been as simple as turning his clothes inside out and putting on a wig. Perhaps he worked the safety chain loose just to make people think he had left the plane. Then he sat down in an empty row.

After the plane landed, he melted into the crowd.

It's a wild idea—but it just might be the truth.

If ever a ship was jinxed, it was the *Amazon.* Its first captain died before it ever hit the water. The second skipper didn't even get the ship out of the harbor. He rammed a dock and sank two little boats. He was fired. The third skipper did better. He sailed the *Amazon* all the way across the Atlantic. When he reached England, he crashed into another ship. He, too, was fired. The fourth skipper sailed the ship back to Canada. There he ran the ship onto a beach by accident. He was asked to look for other work.

The owners decided to sell the ship. Who could blame them? The new owners included sea captain Benjamin Briggs. He planned to skipper the ship himself. Briggs was a clean-living man. He rarely drank. He read the Bible to his sailors every day. He was a very good sailor. Yet he had a hard time rounding up a crew. That's because stories were going around about the ship. Sailors were saying the *Amazon* was cursed. So Briggs and his partners changed the name of the ship to the *Mary Celeste.* Then they were able to hire a crew.

The captain decided to take his wife and daughter along on his first voyage in 1872. The night before he set off, Captain Briggs went ashore. He ran into his friend David Morehouse. This fellow was captain of a ship called the *Dei Gratia.* The two men had dinner together. Morehouse asked Briggs if he had found a

good crew. Briggs answered that it was his best crew ever.

Both ships sailed out the next day. About a month later, Morehouse and his men spotted a dark hulk far away. They set off flares but got no answer. They sailed closer. The dark hulk turned out to be the *Mary Celeste.*

Sailors from the *Dei Gratia* went onto the ship. It was in good shape. The decks were washed. The kitchen was clean. The dishes were all put away. The cargo was stored in the hold. The crew's clothes and goods were on board, right down to their watches and shoes.

The Mary Celeste

The people were missing, however. One lifeboat was gone, too. So were the compasses and maps. The ship's log was lying open in the captain's room. The last line in it read: "About 110 miles due west of the island of Santa Maria." That line had been written ten days earlier. But the date of that line does not tell us when the ship was abandoned. A captain does not write in the log every day. The *Mary Celeste* could have been abandoned only hours before it was found. Indeed, some people said the food in the dining room was still warm. But this story was not true.

Captain Morehouse had a few of his men sail the *Mary Celeste* to a place called Gibraltar. There, the British navy put Morehouse on trial. They said he himself had wrecked the *Mary Celeste.* They said he and his sailors had killed the people on the *Mary Celeste.* But the navy could not prove this idea. No sign of fighting was found on the ship. There were no bodies and no blood. No furniture was overturned. Nothing was broken. None of the *Dei Gratia* sailors would admit to any crime. They all told the same story. At last, the navy had to agree that

Morehouse was telling the truth.

Many guesses have been made about the *Mary Celeste*. Some say people left the ship because a huge storm blew up. But why would sailors leave a big ship in a tiny boat to escape a storm?

Others say a giant sea monster rose from the deep. It stuck its tentacles over the side of the ship. It grabbed people off one by one. But how could it do this without breaking anything or leaving traces of blood? And why was the lifeboat missing? Would people leave a big ship in a tiny boat to escape a sea monster? That is not very likely, either.

Here is another theory. Bread sometimes gets a kind of mold on it called ergot. This mold can kill people. Before they die, however, they see things that are not there. Perhaps the bread on the *Mary Celeste* got this mold on it. Maybe all the people on the ship ate that bread one night. About an hour later, they would all have gone crazy. They might have thought they saw monsters crawling over the ship. They might have seen a lovely island that was not really there. But could a bunch of crazy people get a lifeboat into the water? Would they have the good sense to take their maps and compasses? It's hard to believe.

Yet, if this theory is wrong, the question remains: Why did the people leave the *Mary Celeste* in such a hurry? And where did they go?

In the year 1888, a mysterious
disappearance took place in France. That
year, there was a world fair in Paris. It

The Englishwoman and Her Daughter

was called the Great Exposition. World fairs were very popular at that time. People came to such fairs to look at new products, such as telephones. The Great Exposition was the greatest fair of them all. That is why thousands of people had come to Paris that summer.

Two of the thousands had come all the way from India. One of them was a middle-aged Englishwoman. The other was her daughter, a grown-up young woman. The records no longer tell us their names. They had two rooms waiting for them at a nice hotel in Paris. They had written to the hotel ahead of time to get these rooms. This was very wise, because

every hotel in Paris was jammed that month.

The two women were tired when they arrived. They had been traveling by train for days. They decided to wait until the next morning to see the fair. They wanted only to rest that afternoon.

They signed the guest book. The mother signed on one line, and her daughter signed on the next line down. Then they went upstairs. The mother had been given Room 342. The daughter had the room next door, but she helped her mother settle in first.

Room 342 was really very lovely. The

plum-colored curtains looked fine against the rose wallpaper. The handsome sofa matched the satinwood table. The girl was also struck by the tall brass clock.

Then, suddenly, her mother clutched her stomach. Her face went pale. She fell onto the bed. Her daughter rushed to her side and pressed her hands.

"Get a doctor," the older woman gasped.

It turned out that the hotel had a doctor on its staff. He rushed up to see the Englishwoman. The news was not good. "Your mother is very ill," he told the girl. "She will need some medicine at once.

You must get it, because I have to stay here by her side."

He wrote down the address for her. The girl rushed out, but she was in a strange city. She was young. The streets were crowded. She did not speak French well. It took her four hours to get the medicine and get back to the hotel. By then it was evening. The lobby looked dark and empty. She called for the manager. He came out, wiping his hands on a cloth.

"How is my mother?" she cried out wildly.

The manager stared at her. "What

mother? You came here alone."

The girl's face went white. "But my mother is in Room 342!"

"No. A French family has been in that room all week," said the manager. He took out the hotel guest book. The girl opened it. She found her own name just as she had written it. She could see that it was her own handwriting. But a stranger's name appeared above hers. Another stranger's name appeared below it. All three were written in ink. Nothing had been rubbed out that she could see.

The girl wanted to see Room 342. The manager sighed, but the French family happened to be out just then. So, the manager agreed to let this English girl have just a quick look. He took her up to the third floor and opened up Room 342.

The girl gasped. The room looked completely different. The rose wallpaper was gone. So were the purple curtains. She saw no sofa, no satinwood table, and

no clock. There were clothes she had never seen on the floor.

The hotel doctor was called upstairs. He was puzzled at the girl's questions. He said he had never seen her before. He had certainly not taken care of her "mother."

At last, the girl gave up and went home. There was nothing else she could do.

How can this strange disappearance be explained? Surely someone was lying. Was it the staff at the hotel? But what reason would they have had to lie? How could they have changed the room so much in just four hours? How did they get

rid of the mother's signature? If they simply switched to a new book, how did they get the girl's handwritten signature into it?

Perhaps the girl was lying. Perhaps she really did arrive at the hotel alone. It may be that the two women left India together. The mother then took off for some other country. There, perhaps, she started a new life. The daughter went on to Paris. She made up a story about her mother vanishing. The French police would not keep looking for a stranger who disappeared in their city. The Indian police would not search for a woman who had disappeared on another continent.

That might be one way to explain this disappearance. Perhaps you can think of some other ways.

Many people have disappeared when no one was looking. Some of those cases are very baffling. But the case of David

David Lang

Lang beats them all. Here was a man who vanished in front of five witnesses.

Let's look at the "known" facts. David Lang was a farmer. He owned a patch of land about 12 miles from Gallatin, Tennessee. On September 12, 1880, Lang woke up early and did his usual farm chores. He milked the cow. He fed the chickens. After breakfast, he went out to his fields and finished up his day's work. There wasn't much to do. At this time of year, the farmers were just waiting for their crops to get ripe.

It had been a hot, dry summer. Early afternoon found Lang and his family

relaxing outdoors. David and his wife were sitting on the porch. They were sipping lemonade and brushing away flies. Their children were playing in the small yard below the porch. George was nine now. Sarah was eleven. The yard ran to the edge of a 40-acre pasture.

Beyond the pasture ran the road to Gallatin.

David Lang

The Langs had a good view of it from their porch. They saw a buggy coming from town. It was carrying two men. One was Lang's brother-in-law. The other was a local judge named August Peck. He was a friend of the Lang family.

David Lang set down his lemonade. He started across the pasture to greet his visitors. About halfway across that dusty field, he stopped and turned. His face looked twisted with effort. His mouth moved, but Mrs. Lang heard nothing.

Then it happened. David Lang vanished like a soap bubble. His wife let out a cry and jumped to her feet. The

judge scrambled down from his buggy. All three adults rushed to the spot where Lang had been. They thought he had fallen into a well or something. But when they reached the spot, they found only hard, flat earth. They poked at the grass. It did not give way.

Mrs. Lang fainted. She was carried into the farmhouse. The judge went off to sound the alarm. Neighbors and friends gathered from miles around. They searched Lang's fields and combed through the nearby woods. They found no trace of the man. Scientists later drilled here and there around the field, looking for signs of an underground cave. But there was solid rock under the rich, black soil.

Winter came, and people stopped searching for David Lang. His family went on living in the farmhouse. They got few visitors. Local folks were a little frightened of the farm and its eerie silence.

The next spring, green grass grew in the pastures of Tennessee. But in David Lang's field, something strange happened. Just where he had disappeared, a new kind of grass sprouted. It was tough and coarse, and it grew quickly. Soon a circle of tall brown grass marked the famous spot. It

was 20 feet across. The cows never cropped it or wandered into it. Insects did not fly over it. Nothing seemed to live inside it. Nothing could be heard near that circle except the wind.

About a year after Lang's disappearance, his children walked into that circle one day. They just decided to do it. At the very center of the circle, they held hands. Sarah called out, "Father, are you there?"

Then George joined in. "Father! Answer us!"

And their father did. They heard his voice moaning, "Help me!"

They looked around—they were alone in the circle. Only their father's voice was with them. "Help me," he called again.

The children raced home, frightened but excited. "It's father," they screamed. They dragged their mother by the hand. Mrs. Lang followed them to the field. She, too, called out. And she, too, heard her husband's voice. Now she sent for the neighbors. Search parties formed. People and dogs combed the area. Day after day, David Lang's family camped in the brown circle. Day after day, they called to him. And he answered them. But each day his voice grew fainter, as if he were moving away. And, one day, they could no longer hear him at all.

Mrs. Lang had a nervous breakdown. She rented the farm to Judge Peck. She moved into town with her children. The brown circle faded over time. Ordinary grass took its place. Nothing was ever heard from David Lang again.

Where do you suppose he went?

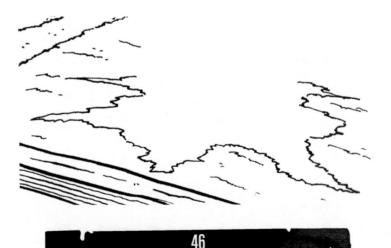

n 1587, a small group of people landed on Roanoke Island near North Carolina. They were the first English settlers in

America. They built a little village on the island. But the colonists soon realized they were in trouble. They needed more supplies to survive in this wilderness. Their leader, John White, agreed to go back to England and get more supplies. With luck, he would be back in three months. White left behind his whole family. They included his newborn granddaughter, Virginia Dare.

The rest of this story is very sad.

John White ran short of money. It took him a year to buy two ships and load them with supplies. Just as he was setting sail, the queen's officers stopped him. England

happened to be at war with Spain just then. The queen decided every English ship had to join the navy. White found himself sailing to war instead of to America. His ships were sunk. He lost all his goods. He dragged himself back to England and started over.

This time it took him a year and a half to scrape together the supplies. He could not buy a ship, but he hired a pirate named John Watts to take him to America.

Hiring a pirate may not sound wise, but White had little choice. In those days, pirates were the best sailors around. And besides, it was safer to sail with a pirate

than without one.

John White gave "his" pirate a lot of money to take him to Roanoke Island. Halfway across the ocean, the pirate changed his mind. He decided to sail to the West Indies instead. He spent many months there, chasing after Spanish ships. Most of them were carrying gold from America to Spain. The pirate sank these ships and took their gold when he could. Finally, in July, he needed a rest. He agreed to sail to Roanoke Island.

Three years had passed since John

White had seen his family. His heart was thumping as he landed on Roanoke Island. He saw smoke rising far away. His heart began to sing. Surely the smoke was a signal from his people. They were alive—they had to be. White and his men moved through the woods, but the smoke was rising from an empty field struck by lightning. There were no people there. The village was gone. In its place stood a fort made of tree trunks. Inside the fort was an empty yard. The houses had been carefully taken apart. The colonists' goods had been removed. Just outside the fort, White found three letters carved into a tree—CRO.

Inside the fort he found a post with the word CROATOAN. That's when White remembered something. About 25 miles down the coast, there was a place called Croatoan Island. The word on the post had to be a message. Surely it meant the colonists had moved to Croatoan Island.

John White reported this happy news to Captain Watts. But Watts had grown impatient. He wanted to go sack some more Spanish ships. John White had waited three years. He was only 25 miles from his family. But he could not talk the pirate into taking him those last few miles. He watched sadly as Roanoke Island shrank in the distance. A few days later, a storm blew the ship off course. It ended up back in England. This broke John White's hopes for good. He gave up on America. He never saw his family again. He died a few years later in Ireland.

No one knows what happened to the colonists of Roanoke. At first, most people thought they must have starved to death or gotten killed by Indians. But over time, people saw that this could not be true. No bones or

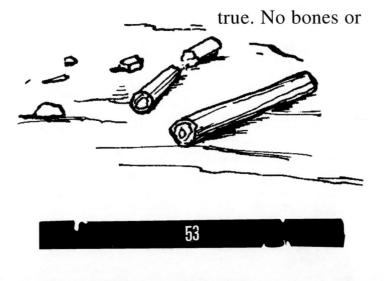

graves were found at Roanoke. Clearly, the colonists had moved. But where?

In 1608, another English colony was planted in America. It was called Jamestown. One of its leaders was Captain John Smith. He was caught by the Indian chief Powhatan. The chief's brother looked at Smith and said, "I have seen others who look like you." He said a whole group of such people were living about five days' journey away. He must have been talking about the lost colony.

After Smith was set free, he tried to find the lost colonists. But the Indians would not help him. Smith gave up his

search. However, an English explorer later found an odd Indian village. It had two-story houses made of stone. It looked like an English town. Yet only Indians seemed to live there. The explorer could never find this town again to prove what he had seen.

Some experts believed the Lumbee Indians of Maryland are descended from the lost colonists. Many of them have gray eyes and light brown hair. Their language seems to include some bits of English. In 1880, a man studied Lumbee names. He found out something very odd. Many Lumbee names resembled family names of the lost colonists. In fact, out of 95 family names in the lost colony, about 45 match up to Lumbee names. Could this be just chance? Or does it tell us what really happened to the Roanoke Colony?